Journey to Wellness

Becoming a Better You

by

LaTonya R. Gaston
MSMHC, LCPCI

Journey to Wellness | *Becoming a Better You*
82pp. ISBN 978-0-578-75871-8
© 2020 by **Unrelenting Media, Inc.**

Published by:

Unrelenting Media, Inc.
c/o *Joseph C. Abraham*
P.O. Box 270065
Las Vegas, NV 89127-0065
http://unrelentingmedia.com
joseph@unrelentingmedia.com

TABLE OF CONTENTS

BIOGRAPHY | LATONYA R. GASTON, MSMHC, LCPCI

LaTonya R. Gaston, MSMHC, LCPCI has a Master of Science in Mental Health Counseling and a Bachelor of Science in Criminal Justice Administration. She has worked as a Clinical Professional Counselor Intern (CPCI) for the State of Nevada for five years under supervision. Throughout her journey as a CPCI, she has made it her priority to maintain a trusting, therapeutic relationship with clients. She is currently employed at Elements of Motivation, where she provides individual psychotherapy. It is her belief that, in order to see change, one must be willing to invest the time and effort to obtain change.

LaTonya is the eldest daughter of Pastors Rose and the late Dr. Bishop Frank Gaston. She has two beautiful children, Aarione Marie, 22, and Zane Brian, 12. She recently became a proud Glamma of Kai Amari, one year. She is a faithful member of God's House International Ministries where she serves in the Praise team and Mental Wellness Department as Head Clinician. She has a passion to help the community become in tune with its higher self by breaking the chains of anxiety, depression, and unresolved trauma through utilizing available resources.

While working her passion on purpose, she created a mental wellness support group on Facebook named "Tonya Talks Mental Health". The platform was created with the community in mind to increase its awareness regarding mental health issues and stigmas that prevent us from seeking adequate help. She believes that her God-given assignment is to help others reach their full potential and maintain mental wellness by accessing available tools to eliminate barriers.

WWW.LATONYAGASTON.COM

PLEDGE | My commitment to heal ME.

I am willing and ready to learn to stop avoiding, denying, and struggling with my inner emotions and, instead, accept that these deeper feelings are appropriate responses to certain situations that should not prevent me from moving forward in my life. With this understanding, I will begin to accept my issues and hardships and commit to making necessary changes in my thoughts and behaviors by doing my healing work, regardless of what is going on in my life, and how others may feel about it.

SIGNED: _____ DATE: _____

This book is dedicated to my father, the late Dr. Bishop Frank Gaston:

Daddy, I will never forget your ambition and drive to succeed throughout many obstacles. To honor you, I live each day as if it is my last. To honor you, I smile more and appreciate each moment spent with those I love. To honor you, Daddy, I work harder to increase the community's awareness of suicide and mental illness. I will be forever grateful to God for your life and legacy. Daddy, you will be missed forever.

Love you forever,
TonPonya

I would like to say thank you to my wonderful support circle who carried, encouraged and uplifted me throughout my own journey to wellness and healing.

To my children, Aarione and Zane:

You are both my reason for striving to be the best mother and person that I can possibly be. You are the wind beneath my wings, and I will forever love you with every fiber in my soul. Thank you for being the best gifts given to me.

To my Mommy dearest, Rose Gaston:

I love your entire life! Thank you for being the best example of true perseverance and strength. Your support, love, and patience with me is appreciated every single day of my life.

To my siblings, Mahogany and Frank Gaston:

I love you and thank you for loving me through it all.

WWW.LATONYAGASTON.COM

DAY 1: It's ok not to be OKAY!
Word of the day: ACCEPTANCE

Is your heart broken and shattered as a result of a death or loss of a loved one, loss of a job, failed friendship, relationship, or marriage? Are you angry because you feel that someone has wronged you? I am here to let you know,

IT IS OK, NOT TO BE OKAY!

Disappointment hurts! Death of a loved one, hurts! Loss of a job, hurts! Pain does not feel good! Please allow me to encourage you to feel what you feel. Take the time you need to heal! If you need support, reach out for help. Remember you are responsible for **YOU**! Trouble doesn't last forever; the sun will shine again! There is a lifeline, but you must reach for it. Everything you need to be well and whole resides inside of you. Tap into your inner resources and refuse to be stuck!

"Say it until you see it" affirmations:

No matter what it looks like, I will be okay.

This is an opportunity for me to grow.

I can experience my feelings in healthy ways.

COMPLETE THE EXERCISE ON PAGE 18

WWW.LATONYAGASTON.COM

JOURNAL PROMPT

I will show myself grace by :

_____

_____

_____

_____

_____

_____

_____

_____

_____

_____

_____

_____

_____

LaTonya R. Gaston

DAY 2: All energy is not good energy.
Word of the day: **VITALITY**

Be careful of the connections you make because not all energy is good, and some could potentially be harmful to your mental health! It is okay to ask people who wish to enter your life their intentions. Seek to understand the purpose for their entrance. If their purpose brings confusion, sadness, and other negative energy, please show them the exit door. Please protect your peace and energy by guarding your mental space. Your mental health depends on you making good decisions that will not only satisfy your mind and body but benefit your life!

"Say it until you see it" affirmations:

I realize what I breathe life into will live, and what I do not will die.

I will breathe in good energy.

I will protect my energy.

COMPLETE THE EXERCISE ON PAGE 20

REPEAT AND COMPLETE

I will protect my energy today by :

_____

_____

_____

_____

_____

_____

_____

_____

_____

_____

_____

_____

LaTonya R. Gaston

DAY 3: Welcome Back!
Word of the day: RESTORATION

Trauma and life have changed you and you may find yourself looking in the mirror to find the person you once were. The beautiful flower was hidden behind hurt, pain, and disappointment. Gather the strength to peel back the layers and say hello to the improved **YOU**! Embrace the journey of learning about who you are NOW as a result of the traumatic experience. There comes a time where you must smack yourself in the face and say, "I am better than this!" I was not created to be miserable. I was fearfully and wonderfully created, and my life matters regardless of my circumstances.

I understand being lost in pain causes you to feel inadequate, unlovable, and unworthy. Allow me to encourage you to believe differently because you deserve love, acceptance and support. The **NEW YOU** should not tolerate, entertain or engage in the foolery of the past. **P.S. WELCOME BACK, YOU WERE MISSED!**

Say it until you see it' affirmations:

I accept that I am bruised but I am not broken.

I am stronger than my circumstances.

I am an overcomer!

COMPLETE THE EXERCISE ON PAGE 22

WWW.LATONYAGASTON.COM

REPEAT AND COMPLETE

This experience has taught me :

_____

_____

_____

_____

_____

_____

_____

_____

_____

_____

_____

LaTonya R. Gaston

DAY 4: Take Heed.
Word of the day: FOCUS

Be mindful when sharing your goals, dreams, and aspirations with others because everybody is **NOT** in your corner! Watch out for people who don't have clear vision (haters) because they may be goal thieves, dream bashers and aspiration killers!! I know you want to feel supported and appreciated, however just be mindful of those you allow in your space and invite to experience your energy. **#TAKEHEED**

Things to remember:

1. *Creating realistic and measurable goals increase the chances of achievement.*

2. *Only share your goals with people who support and believe in your capabilities.*

3. *Be kind to yourself if you make a mistake.*

COMPLETE THE EXERCISE ON PAGE 24

JOURNAL PROMPT

Write five measurable goals that you plan to achieve this year:

1. _____

2. _____

3. _____

4. _____

5. _____

"Take heed, never take advantage of the things you need, never let yourself be overcome by greed; walk the straight and narrow and you shall succeed."
~Shaggy

LaTonya R. Gaston

DAY 5: Guard your mouth.
Word of the day: **SAFEGUARD**

Ways to Guard your Mouth in order to protect your energy and set the tone for your day:

1. *Please don't seek to get into arguments and conflicts with others.*

2. *Learn and practice healthy problem-solving skills.*

3. *Refrain from speaking negatively about yourself and others.*

4. *Cease from judging yourself so harshly and engaging in negative self-talk.*

5. *Speak positive things and affirmations over your life and day.*

Formula for **POSITIVITY**:

Positive thoughts = Positive **MIND**

Positive mind = Positive **VIBES**

Positive Vibes= Positive **DAY/LIFE**

COMPLETE THE EXERCISE ON PAGE 26

JOURNAL PROMPT

List 10 positive words that describe you :

1. _____

2. _____

3. _____

4. _____

5. _____

6. _____

7. _____

8. _____

9. _____

10. _____

"Whoever guards his mouth preserves his life;
he who opens wide his lips comes to ruin."
- Proverbs 13:3

LaTonya R. Gaston

DAY 6: STOP!
Word of the Day: **STANDSTILL**

Many times, we are rushing through life so fast that we forget to see the beauty it brings. It is so important that we **STOP** and take a moment to breathe. **STOP** and look around so that you won't miss the bigger picture. **STOP** thinking that if you suppress your problems long enough that they will somehow dissipate. **STOP** creating false narratives in order to avoid the truth! **STOP** underestimating your capabilities and greatness. **STOP** trying to impress people who don't care about you anyway. Just **STOP**! Remember you have the power to put an end to the majority of your problems if you would just take a moment to **STOP**!

Things to remember:

1. *You have the power to change your perspective.*

2. *Taking time to process is beneficial in gaining a greater sense of understanding.*

3. *Do not get stuck in the process.*

COMPLETE THE EXERCISE ON PAGE 28

JOURNAL PROMPT

My previous negative experience could have been different if I would have :

_____

_____

_____

_____

_____

_____

_____

_____

_____

_____

_____

_____

LaTonya R. Gaston

DAY 7: Speak life.
Word of the day: WHOLENESS

The challenge today is for you to speak life into your life! If you feel your spark has died due to circumstances and unfortunate situations, let me encourage you to **SPEAK LIFE** into your motivation! If you feel your energy is completely depleted due to overextending your time, effort, and resources, **SPEAK LIFE** into your energy and maintain healthy boundaries! If you feel you have lost the ability to love and trust due to involvement in toxic relationships, **SPEAK LIFE** into your heart. In fact, you are still capable of loving and trusting again! **SPEAK LIFE** into your present and future because you have everything you need inside of you to have a blessed and bountiful **LIFE! SPEAK LIFE AND LIVE!**

"Say it until you see it" affirmations:

I am not my experiences, but they have taught very valuable lessons.

I have a wealth of love, life, and peace that the world needs.

I am capable of loving and being loved.

COMPLETE THE EXERCISE ON PAGE 30

JOURNAL PROMPT

The thing that surprises me about my life is :

_____

_____

_____

_____

_____

_____

_____

_____

_____

_____

_____

_____

_____

LaTonya R. Gaston

DAY 8: Feed your soul.
Word of the day: **PURPOSE**

Feeding your soul is so much more than just doing what makes you feel good. Purchasing a blouse or a pair of Jordans on sale can make you feel good. It helps to be aware of the fact that you are indeed a **SOUL** first, placed on Earth to complete a mission. When you do your work to accomplish goals on your life's journey, you are feeding your soul. Believe it or not, you don't have to be super **SAVED** or religious for this to happen. God is in your life regardless of if you want to recognize His presence or not. Work genuinely to align the soul of your spirit with the essence of who you are. Tap into your hidden treasures and bring forth your God-given purpose to be fulfilled on the Earth, in this your soul can be truly fed.

"Say it until you see it" affirmations:

I will give myself the necessary time and space to grow and stretch.

I can manifest success, happiness, and peace.

I will feed my soul by trusting my healing journey.

COMPLETE THE EXERCISE ON PAGE 32

JOURNAL PROMPT

I forgive myself for not being open to receive :

_____

_____

_____

_____

_____

_____

_____

_____

_____

_____

_____

LaTonya R. Gaston

DAY 9: Always be ready to do your work.
Word of the day: BENEVOLENCE

While sitting at the pedicure bar, a young man enters and comes to sit in the booth next to me. He appeared down and anxious as evidenced by his body language and facial expression. I redirected my focus and continued enjoying my **SELF-CARE** and then he said, "Do you go to church, and can you pray for me?"

I answered, "Yes".

He begins to cry and says, "I need help."

Because I am God's helper and healer, I say, "How can I help you?"

He begins to shake uncontrollably in the massage chair. I proceed to speak softly and use mindfulness techniques so he can relax.

He said, "I need a therapist because I am really going through so much."

I say well today is your blessed day, because I can pray for you and I am a therapist.

This experience taught me that I must always be ready to serve and do my work because you just never know when someone needs you. Although I have made mistakes and sometimes have doubted my worth, someone still needed my light. My hope for you is that you never miss your opportunity to shine bright, first in your life, but as well as in the lives of others.

WWW.LATONYAGASTON.COM

Things to Remember:

1.   Be a **LIGHT**, *because you never know who needs your energy to* **SHINE**.

2.   *Be careful of judging a book by its cover, because you may miss your opportunity to do your healing work.*

3.   *Kindness travels further than hatred.*

JOURNAL PROMPT

Reflect on a loving way that you helped someone recently and journal about how you can do the same for yourself.

_____

_____

_____

_____

_____

_____

_____

LaTonya R. Gaston

DAY 10: Be grateful.
Word of the day: GRATITUDE

In my experience, I have found that it is really important that we spend more time focusing on what we have and who is important to us instead of catastrophizing what could happen. Be grateful for what is and try not to put any energy into what is not. Depression and anxiety set in when we focus on what we do not possess. Positive thoughts and acts are results of displaying gratitude. Take a moment to reflect on all the wins in your life, celebrate them and smile.

Things to Remember:

1. *Be grateful for where you are on your journey to wellness.*

2. *No matter how small the accomplishment it still counts as a win.*

3. *Be proud of your motivation and willingness to continue despite the challenges.*

COMPLETE THE EXERCISE ON PAGE 37

LaTonya R. Gaston

JOURNAL PROMPT

List 9 things you are grateful for today :

1. _____

2. _____

3. _____

4. _____

5. _____

6. _____

7. _____

8. _____

9. _____

DAY 11: Renew, refresh, and replenish.
Word of the Day: REFRESH

Renew your mind daily by emptying out the negative thoughts of yesterday. Start over and forget what triggered an emotional response. Breathe deeply and take in positive and clean energy. Be diligent to use your **WISE** mind to make decisions. Be confident and consistent and try not to entertain toxic people, patterns or behaviors. Protect your mind by listening only to conversations that are full of substance. Take time throughout your day to rest your mind by closing out everything around you for a moment of peace during a lunch break.

The Wise Mind is the portion of the mind that aligns our inside knowledge, intuition, emotional thinking mind, and rational thinking mind together to help us accept the truth. Our wise mind is like the calm after the storm or the part of the mind that just knows the truth. The wise mind helps you to rationalize and see the bigger picture. The wise mind seeks peace and resolution. My hope for you is that you would stop and think before you respond. My prayer is that you would be guided by your **WISE** mind!

Repeat and Complete:

I will make a genuine effort to **RENEW** *my mind daily by* :

_____

_____

LaTonya R. Gaston

I will make a genuine effort to **REFRESH** *my heart by getting rid of* :

_____

_____

I will make a genuine effort to **REPLENISH** *my body by* :

_____

_____

"A mind that is stretched by new experiences
can never go back to its old dimensions." ~
Oliver Wendell Holmes

The sentiments of my heart :

_____

_____

_____

_____

_____

_____

DAY 12: Time is non-refundable.
Word of the day: AWARENESS

As you embark on this new day, please take a moment to bask on the precious gift of life! Certainly, tomorrow is not promised, so it is important that you live each day as if it was your last, be authentic and accepting of who you truly are, not who you want to be. Cherish those that have entered and exited your life and be thankful for those experiences. Close your eyes and take a moment to inhale and breathe in the beauty of this moment and exhale the doubt of what you are not. Living in your present moment protects your energy and prevents symptoms of anxiety to cloud your body. Embrace the moment of peace, this day will never come again. Close all the open tabs in your mind and just be… Focus on today and live in the power of **NOW**.

"Say it until you see it" affirmations:

I will not focus on the pain and disappointment of yesterday.

I am aware and in tune with self.

I will value my time, energy, and efforts.

COMPLETE THE EXERCISE ON PAGE 41

LaTonya R. Gaston

JOURNAL PROMPT

What area of your life have you taken for granted?

_____

_____

_____

_____

_____

_____

How will you be more considerate of yourself?

_____

_____

_____

_____

_____

_____

_____

DAY 13: Believe only the truth about you!
Word of the day: CONFIDENCE

Make it a practice to only believe what God says about you. Be mindful of people who try to plant negative, sabotaging seeds to discount your worth and esteem.

For a moment, take into consideration the people who have attacked your confidence and realize they are not qualified to tell you how to feel about yourself. Their negative opinions about you are inaccurate, invalid and unimportant. You must always be aware and on guard to protect **SELF**.

Food for thought: Just because someone develops an opinion of you does not make it a fact! Always remember that God never changes how He feels about you. He loves regardless of your choices and insecurities.

Do not engage in self-sabotaging behaviors that change your view of yourself. Only believe what is true about you. Many people experience low self-esteem or lack confidence for various reasons, but this does not have to be you. Listen, if someone continuously beats you down with negative and damaging comments causing you to feel down about yourself, please release them and let them go! Have a letting-go party and work diligently to heal.

"Say it until you see it" affirmations:

I vow to believe only the truth about myself.

I am beautiful!

LaTonya R. Gaston

I am qualified!

I am justified and your approval isn't needed.

JOURNAL PROMPT

What is the truth about you that you wish everyone knew?

_____

_____

_____

_____

_____

_____

_____

_____

_____

_____

_____

DAY 14: Listen to your body.
Word of the day: **OBSERVANT**

On December 31st, I experienced the worst tooth pain ever. I thought to myself, "This is not how I want to start 2020." So, I discovered that I had to have oral surgery which would prevent me from working. Thank God everything went well, and I healed appropriately. It is crazy how things happen to force you to get rest. I did not notice how much I needed that time of recovery to not only rest, but to reset! I am grateful for this experience because, had it not happened this way, I would not have taken days off work to care for myself! I believe in self-care and I practice it on a regular basis but sometimes I fail to listen to the number one indicator, my body! Let me encourage you to listen and obey the signals that your body gives. It could be a headache, back pain, or stomach issues whatever it is, **LISTEN** because it is trying to tell you something!

"*Say it until you see it*" affirmations:

I understand that my body is my temple.

Regardless of my circumstances, **I AM ME.**

I own everything about me, my feelings, my words, and all of my actions.

COMPLETE THE EXERCISE ON PAGE 45

LaTonya R. Gaston

JOURNAL PROMPT

As I scan my body, I notice that I am :

_____

_____

_____

_____

_____

_____

_____

_____

_____

_____

_____

_____

DAY 15: It's in the silence.
Word of the day: SERENITY

Shhhh... Are you listening? Can you hear the inner cry in your heart? There is an urgency to be heard, helped, and healed. If you listen closely, you can hear the loudness of the hidden emotional pain that you have once experienced. Maybe you are sitting in the seat of emotional turmoil filled with abandonment, neglect, and fear. Listen to yourself instead of judging and placing inappropriate blame on others. Have you considered that your **"INNER ME"** has become the **"ENEMY"**? I know you may feel there is no way out and your options are limited, but the way of escape has already been provided and it's in the silence.

Seek to understand instead of blaming and defaming. The silent cry is where your focus should be. You see, it is in the silence that lives are lost, and irrational decisions are made. Please make a conscious effort to be a part of the solution that helps to eliminate the problem. I urge you to refuse to suffer in silence! Have a sit down with yourself and explore what you truly need to be well. There is help and you can be healed if you want it!

"Say it until you see it" affirmations:

I will release the matters of my heart in order to heal.

I will align myself with a circle of support to assist through my healing journey.

COMPLETE THE EXERCISE ON PAGE 47

LaTonya R. Gaston

JOURNAL PROMPT

What message is your heart conveying? And how will you begin doing your healing work?

_____

_____

_____

_____

_____

_____

_____

_____

_____

_____

_____

_____

DAY 16: Feelings . . . .
Word of the Day: **STILLNESS**

> *"Feelings, so deep in my feelings*
> *No, this ain't really like me*
> *Can't control my anxiety*
> *Feelings."*
> ~Ella Mae

Tips for dealings with feelings:

1. *Sit with your emotions by identifying what you're experiencing without judging yourself.*

UNHEALTHY: *"I shouldn't be crying; I am so weak!"*

HEALTHY: It is **OK** to feel without criticizing and judging yourself.

2. *Validating your emotions means accepting them.*

UNHEALTHY: Suppressing and avoiding feelings by excessively engaging in self harming and sabotaging behaviors.

HEALTHY: *"I am really angry right now."*

Please Continue to the next page. This space is intentionally left blank.

LaTonya R. Gaston

3. *Focus on the* **NOW**, *instead of being stuck in your experience.*

UNHEALTHY: *"I just can't get over you lying to me, this ruined my entire day,"*

HEALTHY: When the feeling of anger resurfaces, address the person by dealing with the action that triggered the emotion, and let go so that you can heal.

Sitting in your emotions may be uncomfortable, however it is a skill that can be learned and practiced.... You've got this!

"Say it until you see it" affirmations:

I will give myself permission to experience my feelings as they come.

I will be gentle with myself and allow my feelings to be expressed in healthy ways.

I am in charge of how I feel and in control of my emotions.

What is one word that describes how you are currently feeling?

_____

_____

_____

_____

_____

_____

DAY 17: Forgive yourself.
Word of the Day: **GRACE**

I would like to encourage you to forgive yourself for making mistakes, for being unaware, and trusting the wrong people. It is important to know that unresolved hurt creates bitterness and insecurity. Don't lose focus of the goal to "**HEAL THY SELF!**"

You are deserving of forgiveness and you owe it to yourself to release the pain that you have carried for so long. God has forgiven you and He wants to live an abundant life full of joy and peace. Today is the day to walk in your healing and forgive in order to live free. Give yourself the grace and forgiveness that you so freely give to everyone else.

My hope is that you learn to forgive yourself so that you can walk and live in your true healing. My prayer for you is that you begin to accept your truth and embrace the freedom to live a free life full of love, light, self-control, increased knowledge, and peace.

Things to remember:

1. *You are stronger than your past.*

2. *Failing to forgive yourself and others prevents you from fully healing.*

3. *Forgiveness releases unwanted burdens and shame.*

COMPLETE THE EXERCISE ON PAGE 51

LaTonya R. Gaston

JOURNAL PROMPT

I forgive myself for :

_____

_____

_____

_____

_____

_____

_____

_____

_____

_____

_____

_____

DAY 18: Be thankful.
Word of the Day: THANKSGIVING

Give yourself a round of applause because you deserve it! Appreciate your progress and the positive steps you've made to get to this point in your life.

Be very kind to yourself and be thankful for **YOU**! You made it despite all the obstacles against you.

Your resilience has increased, and you can bounce back from any challenge.

Be thankful for your experiences because they have provided you with very valuable lessons.

Celebrate your progress and be super proud that you are not who you used to be!

"Say it until you see it" affirmations:

I will be thankful for what is.

I am growing stronger and better because of my experiences.

I am learning to be grateful for what I have while being excited for what is yet to come.

COMPLETE THE EXERCISE ON PAGE 53

LaTonya R. Gaston

REPEAT AND COMPLETE

I intend to align my actions, words, and thoughts to these beliefs :

_____

_____

_____

_____

_____

_____

_____

_____

_____

"I am thankful for my struggle because without it,
I wouldn't have stumbled upon my strength."
~Alexandra Elle

WWW.LATONYAGASTON.COM

DAY 19: Set boundaries.
Word of the Day: LIMITS

No one knows when enough is enough for you. You set the tone for what you will and will not accept. People will only go as far as you allow. Take steps to set healthy boundaries and limitations so that people know how far to go before that have crossed the line. Please do not allow people to upset your spirit today. Reacting after becoming bothered by the actions of others only releases your power and control to the person. Never allow someone to take you away from YOU! "Boundaries give a sense of agency over one's physical space, body, and feelings," says Jenn Kennedy, a licensed marriage and family therapist. "We all have limits, and boundaries communicate that line." Creating healthy boundaries have benefits such as improved self-esteem, increased independence and self-advocacy, and protection of energy and space.

"Say it until you see it" affirmations:

I am in control of who and what I allow in my space.

I understand my personal boundaries and respect the boundaries of others.

I have the power to disagree or say no without guilt.

COMPLETE THE EXERCISE ON PAGE 55

LaTonya R. Gaston

REPEAT AND COMPLETE

In the past, I have released my power to another by :

_____

_____

_____

However, I realize that I am in control and I will not allow others to :

_____

_____

_____

Sentiments of my heart :

_____

_____

_____

_____

_____

DAY 20: What you believe will manifest.
Word of the Day: **BELIEVE**

What you believe will manifest! Therefore, it is so important to think positive, pure, and loving things. **PHILIPPIANS 4:8, KJV** states, "*Finally, brethren, whatsoever things are true, whatsoever things are honest, whatsoever things are just, whatsoever things are pure, whatsoever things are lovely, whatsoever things are of good report; if there be any praise, think on these things.*"

I know this may be difficult at times; however, it is doable! Just believe, despite what it looks like. What are you feeding your mind? Hate, negativity, and self-sabotaging thoughts? Well, stop it! Your mind is a powerful thing to waste. Haven't you heard, "You are what you believe?" Challenge yourself to believe differently today! Manifest positivity, good vibes, success, peace, and wholeness and what you believe you will receive.

COMPLETE THE EXERCISE ON PAGE 57

LaTonya R. Gaston

REPEAT AND COMPLETE

Today, I will intentionally embrace :

_____

_____

_____

_____

_____

_____

_____

_____

_____

_____

_____

_____

DAY 21: Do the right thing.
Word of the Day: INTEGRITY

I do my best to live a life of integrity and good character. I'm not saying that I am perfect because I'm not. However, I make sure when I lay my head down at night that I'm ok with my decisions and I don't have anybody else's blood on my hands. I make it a practice to do right by people not because I expect it back, but because my mom always says that it's just right to do right. I live by this! Although I live by these standards, I cannot expect that everyone else will.

So, I leave you with the great words of **Maria Razumich-Zec**: "Your reputation and integrity are everything. Follow through on what you say you're going to do. Your credibility can only be built over time, and it is built from the history of your words and actions." It is so important that you make a conscious decision to do what feels right to you. Refrain from looking to others to make life changing decisions for you. Trust your inner "dopeness" and exhibit good moral character and integrity.

Things to remember:

1. *Make good on your promises.*

2. *Be accountable to yourself and others.*

3. *Have the courage to say no when necessary.*

COMPLETE THE EXERCISE ON PAGE 59

LaTonya R. Gaston

JOURNAL PROMPT

From this point on, I will tell myself the truth about :

_____

_____

_____

_____

_____

_____

_____

_____

_____

_____

_____

_____

_____

DAY 22: Release and let go.
Word of the Day: **PEACE**

If you would like to embody and experience peace in your heart, you must reveal and uncover the contents in your heart. Empty out hurt, pain, fear, trauma, disappointment, and brokenness. These issues have held you back for so long. When will you release in order to freely experience peace? I challenge you to discard what no longer serves you and brings you peace. Take genuine steps to deal with what is inside so that it does not continue to affect you. Sometimes the toxic person is **YOU**! Tap into your heart and begin to put an end to toxic stress that's beneath your surface!

Release Party Activity:

Tear stripes of paper and write down people/things that have prevented you from experiencing peace. Once written, have a letting go party. You can choose to burn the stripes or throw them away. Whatever you choose, **JUST RELEASE**!

"Say it until you see it" affirmation:

I am at peace.

Peace is in my heart.

I will freely release to experience **PEACE**.

COMPLETE THE EXERCISE ON PAGE 61

LaTonya R. Gaston

JOURNAL PROMPT

I have held _____ *for so long but today I will release.*

Who am I? What do I need to be free and/or at peace?

_____

_____

_____

_____

_____

_____

_____

_____

_____

_____

_____

_____

_____

DAY 23: I am losing me because I am not choosing ME.
Word of the Day: SELF-ADVOCACY

Being shackled and chained down by the burdens of engaging in toxic patterns, relationships, and behaviors can cause you to forget your purpose in life. For over 15 years of my life I was involved in a relationship that webbed feelings of fear, confusion, self-doubt, continuous abandonment, and guilt. I have always believed in love and have held on to the dream of someday finding true love. Every relationship has their share of ups and downs, however when you begin to experience more downs than ups the relationship should call for evaluation.

One day, I felt as if my world had turned upside down. The relationship took a turn for the worst and my partner was taken away from me. I found myself depressed, lonely, helpless, and broken. During this time, I began to isolate from friends and family. I had allowed this situation to overtake my dreams, aspirations and positive outlook on life. This turmoil continued for more than a year, until one day I was on the verge of a nervous breakdown and I reached out for help. I was fearful of being alone and the fear in conjunction with other negative feelings caused me to lose myself. I began to do my healing work with the assistance of prayer, my support circle and my wonderful therapist.

Throughout my journey to healing and wellness, I realized that I had become really good at masking my true feelings. I chose to allow the pain to overshadow me and I had become addicted to my pain and anxiety. I disguised my pain so well in the public, but I would drown myself in tears at home. Until the day of rebirthing and refreshing came and I regained control over my feelings. At that moment, I confessed to losing myself because I failed to choose myself.

LaTonya R. Gaston

The pain that has burdened you may not look like mine, however, allow me to encourage you to choose you instead of losing you in the process. So many times, we want to share in the pain of loved ones dear to us not knowing the potential harm this may bring to you. It is perfectly okay to sympathize and help carry the burden of others. However, it is so important that you do not attempt to OWN the pain of someone else. The consequences of taking ownership of someone else's burden are far more damaging to your wellness than you know.

You must ask yourself, if I become so engulfed in someone's pain, can I sympathize without taking ownership and losing myself? It is extremely important that you maintain healthy boundaries to ensure you are not bogged down with the burdens of others. Allow me to encourage you to take care of yourself by protecting your own feelings and refraining from taking ownership of what does not belong to you.

I AM LOSING ME, BY NOT CHOOSING ME!

I choose to take control of :

1. _____

2. _____

3. _____

I choose to continue my 'Journey to Wellness' by :

1. _____

2. _____

3. _____

Journey to Wellness | *Becoming a Better You*

I choose to use these positive coping tools to help me maintain change :

1. _____

2. _____

3. _____

Sentiments of my heart :

_____

_____

_____

_____

_____

_____

_____

_____

_____

_____

LaTonya R. Gaston

DAY 24: Look up and live.
Word of the Day: **VISUALIZE**

Sometimes life hits us below the belt and causes us to hold our heads down in defeat and disappointment. The challenges and situations on this journey have a way of forcing us to stretch and grow. Acknowledging sadness is a temporary feeling that does not have to affect your entire day. Try taking on a new perspective and realize that this is only a moment of brokenness or sadness.

Remember troubles don't last always. **1 PETER 5:10** encourages us by saying, "The suffering won't last forever. It won't be long before this generous God who has great plans for us in Christ - eternal and glorious plans they are! - will have you put together and on your feet for good." Visualize your next positive moment and be compelled to look up and live!

Things to remember:

1. *To focus on the good things that have happened in your life.*

2. *To find the lesson in your trauma.*

3. *Your mistakes, failures, and disappointments* do NOT *define you!*

4. *New discoveries are pieces of information* NOT *confirmations!*

COMPLETE THE SENTIMENT ON PAGE 66

JOURNAL PROMPT

Sentiments of my heart :

_____

_____

_____

_____

_____

_____

_____

_____

_____

_____

_____

_____

LaTonya R. Gaston

DAY 25: What's in your toolbox?
Word of the Day: ACCESSIBILITY

Did you know that you have everything you need inside of you to be well, healed, and empowered? 2 Timothy 3:17 states, "That the man of God may be perfect, thoroughly equipped for all good works." This scripture encourages us to know that we were provided everything that we need to be great. Many times, circumstances and life's trials beat us down and force us to cover up and hide our tools of success and wellness. What's in your mental health toolbox?

How are you coping with stress, depression, anxiety, and the rest? It is so important to have healthy tools in your box because if you do not, you will develop unhealthy patterns and habits. Healthy tools may include journaling, talking to a mental health therapist, exercising, and psychotropic medication.

Today, I would like for you to confess and say, "I need what I need." Please do not allow shame, embarrassment, and fear to cause you to reject what your body, mind, and heart needs to be fully functional. Help yourself become better by knowing when to access your healthy tools.

COMPLETE THE EXERCISE ON PAGE 68

REPEAT AND COMPLETE

I will access the tools I need to heal and grow.

These are the tools I need to heal and grow :

1. _____

2. _____

3. _____

My support circle :

1. _____

2. _____

3. _____

Sentiments of my heart :

_____

_____

_____

_____

_____

LaTonya R. Gaston

DAY 26: Reveal "It" to heal "It".
Word of the Day: **LIGHT**

As humans we find it so easy to point the finger and call out when someone else is struggling with an issue. However, oftentimes we fail to talk about the pain, trauma, and hidden secrets that we so diligently mask. Those deep dark secrets have invoked pain, trust issues, insecurity, shame, and guilt. Nonetheless, we carry them and instead of healing from the issues we suppress them because it hurts to feel. Allow me to remind you of the commitment that you signed in the beginning of this book to do your healing work.

In order to begin your work, you must reveal issues that have caused you to be complacent and challenged in various areas in your life. You deserve healing and light. You deserve to settle matters of your heart that prevent you from loving freely. You deserve to close chapters of hurt, sadness, trauma, and pain. You owe it to yourself to live a life of joy and abundance. Learning to cope and live through trauma can be difficult work. However, it is possible with motivation and determination to heal. Throughout the healing process it is important that you stay connected to your support circle, embrace the good things in your life, and focus on healing one day at a time.

My prayer for you is that you find a mental health therapist that you can trust with your pain. Someone who will be equally as dedicated to this process as you. I am so elated that you are choosing to live your life differently. My hope is that you become healed and set free from your past by living with and accepting your truth. I believe in your capabilities and I am proud of you for choosing **YOU**!

Things to remember:

1.   *Masking trauma is emotionally exhausting.*

2.   *You are still capable of loving and being loved.*

3.   *Holding on to trauma is painful to you and can affect those around you.*

Reflection Questions:

Where is this pain manifesting in my body? Is there a time or person attached to this pain? How do I plan to heal from this pain?

_____

_____

_____

_____

_____

_____

_____

_____

_____

LaTonya R. Gaston

DAY 27: Do it differently.
Word of The Day: CHANGE

In life we become accustomed to following patterns and routines. As a child of Pastors, I can recall going to church Monday-Sunday and becoming weary with the routine. This healthy habit was the foundation and center of my spiritual walk with Christ. However, there are some patterns and learned behaviors that some of us have continued that are not healthy or conducive to our mental and physical growth. Perhaps, your father abused your mother or there is a generational curse of addiction that runs deep in your family. Please know that these patterns and behaviors can end with you.

This may be your opportunity to vow to do it differently. Refuse to settle with the past, choose a different approach and perspective. You are not your past and the dysfunctional cycle can stop with you! Although choosing to do it differently may sound easy, this process takes your genuine effort to be committed to your change. Choose to love instead of hate. Choose to live and not die. Choose to resolve opposed to regret. Allow me to encourage you to do it differently today. Depression, anxiety, frustration, and emotional stress you will not win today. I am proud of you. Give yourself credit for making such a great decision to choose differently. Remember, you've got this!

Things to Remember:

1. *You have every right to begin again.*

2. *Choosing to remove yourself from situations that are not conducive to your mental wellness is your business.*

LaTonya R. Gaston

3.   *You are courageous and brave for choosing You.*

4.   *Anger, frustration, and worrying are choices, choose different!*

"Choosing a new way means you are learning and accepting that the old way no longer works."
~ LaTonya Gaston

Sentiments of my heart :

_____

_____

_____

_____

_____

_____

_____

_____

_____

_____

DAY 28: Show up for yourself.
Word of The Day: PRESENCE

Many times, we look to others to cheer, boost our esteem, and applaud our efforts and accomplishments. However, it is important that you show up for yourself first before you expect anyone else to be present in your life. When was the last time you gave yourself credit for accomplishing a goal, or gifted yourself by word or deed for saying no without regret? We must learn to celebrate a win whether big or small. I used to be my own worst and most critical enemy until I learned how to show up for myself. Do not get me wrong, it feels good to have people in your corner and the opportunity to have access to an amazing support team.

But, none of that matters if you criticize and fail to believe in your own capabilities. Do you believe that you can do it? I believe in your abilities to always be present for yourself first and then to those connected to you. My prayer for you is that you continue to be emotionally present for You. It is important to know that you are your best advocate. Show up for yourself by paying attention to your body, being determined to meet your own emotional and physical needs. Make yourself a priority every single day.

Things to remember today:

1. *You are worthy of acceptance, love, and support.*

2. *You have the freedom to use your voice.*

3. *You are a good person.*

LaTonya R. Gaston

4. *You should give yourself the love you give to everyone else.*

Repeat and Complete:

I realize that I have allowed people, places, and things to....

_____

_____

_____

_____

_____

_____

_____

_____

_____

_____

_____

_____

DAY 29: Get past your past.
Word of the Day: **EVOLVE**

Oftentimes we get so comfortable in our discomfort and dysfunction that we lose sight of our purpose. During our discomfort and dysfunction, we experience feelings of guilt, disappointment, sadness, and frustration and we begin to hold on to the emotional baggage. This emotional baggage follows us into our occupation, social interactions, relationships, and more. It is important to know that in order to embrace the **NEW** you must release the **OLD**. Allow me to encourage you to release baggage of toxicity, frustration, disappointment, and pain so that you can welcome growth, success, love, and light.

In order to get past your past, the process first must begin in the mind. The mind stores those traumatic and painful memories, which causes us to reflect on the past more often than not. The 90's group EnVogue said it best, "Free your mind and the rest will follow." Renew your mind by changing your thought pattern and refusing to continue being stuck in the emotional web. Next, your body will put things into action. The heart is one of the most important functions of the body and it houses the pain, agony, and despair of the past. Therefore, the heart requires cleansing by identifying and releasing the emotional pain that you have held onto for so long.

Now you are ready to welcome the new because you have gone through a period of reconstruction and rebuilding. You must begin walking with confidence and purpose. This final step involves you holding your head up and realizing that your life is meant to be lived in joy abundantly because God said so. My prayer for you is that you find a mental health therapist that you can trust with

LaTonya R. Gaston

your pain. Someone who will be equally as dedicated to this process as you.

Lastly, be encouraged by one of my favorite scriptures, **ROMANS 8:28**, "And we know that in all things God works for the good of those who love him, who have been called according to his purpose.

Sentiments of my heart :

_____

_____

_____

_____

_____

_____

_____

_____

_____

_____

_____

_____

DAY 30: YOU MADE IT!
Word of the Day: EFFORT

Today is the day of day of completion and finalization. You have made it to the end of this book but certainly not to the end of your journey. I am super proud that you gave yourself the gift of completion. Your journey may have been rocky, weary, and frustrating however none of that even matters because **YOU MADE IT!** Rest your heart and mind. Think happy thoughts and believe that everything is working the way it is supposed to work. Be proud that you didn't give up throughout the process. Count your blessings and every win at the close of each night.

Be reminded of the commitment that you made in the beginning of this book and celebrate your efforts to become a better you. You are stronger than you believed yourself to be. My hope for you is that you continue working on self. I am praying that you have learned to walk fully in your purpose with confidence and security. It is important to realize that challenges and storms will continue to arise however prayerfully now you are equipped with skills and knowledge to confront each situation with grace. Continue to take ownership of your life by speaking positive affirmations over your life.

My hope is that you continue your healing work. My prayer is that you remain responsible for you and that your purpose was discovered throughout this journey. Remember to surround yourself with people who support, uplift, and believe in you. Be mindful and aware by constantly gauging your attitude and motives. Keep healthy boundaries and, most importantly, never be afraid to practice your power of choice. Choose wisely.

LaTonya R. Gaston

Things to Remember:

1.   *You are capable of living the life you want to live.*

2.   *You can do the work you need to do to gain control over your life.*

3.   *You are the author of your story and although the chapters may be full of twists and turns, you have the power to make it a happy ending.*

Sentiments of my heart :

_____

_____

_____

_____

_____

_____

_____

_____

_____

_____

Lightning Source UK Ltd.
Milton Keynes UK
UKHW020842150920
369944UK00012B/638